Sponging

A guide to living off those you love

ANTHONY E. MARSH

JAY BLUMENFIELD

ROBERT MORITZ

HarperPaperbacks
A Division of HarperCollins*Publishers*

HarperPaperbacks   *A Division of* HarperCollins*Publishers*
10 East 53rd Street, New York, N.Y. 10022

Copyright © 1995 by Anthony E. Marsh, Jay Blumenfield, and Robert Moritz
All rights reserved. No part of this book may be used or reproduced in any manner whatsoever without written permission of the publisher, except in the case of brief quotations embodied in critical articles and reviews. For information address HarperCollins*Publishers*, 10 East 53rd Street, New York, N.Y. 10022

HarperPaperbacks may be purchased for educational, business, or sales promotional use. For information, please write: Special Markets Department, HarperCollins*Publishers*, 10 East 53rd Street, New York, N.Y. 10022

A trade paperback edition of this book was published in 1995 by Dune Road Books

Cover photography copyright © 1994 by Dick Richards
Book design by Wendy Wessel and Andrea Reich
Book art by Gordon Jones

First HarperPaperbacks printing: May 1996

Printed in the United States of America

HarperPaperbacks and colophon are trademarks of HarperCollins*Publishers*

10 9 8 7 6 5 4 3 2 1

Dedicated to our ATMs and Dishwashers:
Alan & Judy, Michael & Susan, and Milton & Barbara

Thanks for working hard...
so we didn't have to.

I never think of the future.
It comes soon enough.

-Albert Einstein, December 1930

Contents.

INTRODUCTION.

Who is a Sponger?

A "sponger" is defined in Webster's as "One who habitually depends on others for his/her maintenance." It comes from the Greek *sphongos* meaning soft, tight rear. For most of the twentieth century, spongers have been looked down upon as parasites with no respect for society. Today, however, spongers are a positive and legitimate force, replete with their own values, principles and codes of honor. The modern sponger is a person who finds mainstream life suffocating. This misunderstood entity might be you, it might be a friend, it might be that comatose heap of flesh drooling on your couch right now. The modern sponger is dedicated to the following principle:

SPONGING PRINCIPLE NUMBER ONE

Work output should never equal or, God forbid, exceed the volume of benefits gained. In other words, **"Life's short, work little."**

What is Sponging?

"Sponging" is a celebration of life, liberty, and the pursuit of cable. It is the American dream of a white picket fence, a two-car garage, and a Barca Lounger with rolling heat massage—just without those pesky 9 to 5 hours. It is having your cake and eating it too, then finding someone else to wash the dishes. Many believe sponging represents the greatest career opportunity since Communism. Yet, as you will read, sponging does require some thought. (It also takes a fair amount of vim and vigor, instinct and intuition, Captain and Tenille.)

Where do spongers come from?

Spongers begin in the womb, where all of life's necessities are provided in the blink of a partially formed eye. (NOTE: Statistics have shown that babies delivered cesarean—i.e. those surgically yanked from the womb—grow to be the most successful spongers.)

During childhood, proto-spongers learn life's essential lessons: crying yields a milk-filled nipple, smiling at the doctor yields a tootsie pop and even restraining from carrying-on-'til-you-get-there yields an extra ride on the rollercoaster.

As proto-spongers grow through adolescence, a second womb forms, keeping them warm, well fed and in touch with the prime-time t.v. line-up. But instead of appreciating the beautiful, parasitic balance of this situation, they feel overwhelmed by universal injustice. They have to battle Dad for the remote control. They have to deal with unreasonable responsibility—like throwing furry produce out from under their beds. They have to actually conduct a conversation with their parents more than once a week.

The bottom line: **Living at home sucks**.

Pre-spongers feel compelled to get out and liberate themselves from the pressures and restrictions of parental rule. Yet, sadly, these pre-spongers do not understand that with freedom comes responsibility, with no curfew comes no dinner, with your own space comes your own cable bill. After amassing volumes of case studies, testimonies, statistics and personal pain-staking anecdotes, the authors of this book have come to the following, irrefutable scientific conclusion: **Leaving home sucks more**.

To sponge or not to sponge?

Now it is the time to sit down and contemplate. Talk to friends. Consult a Magic Eight Ball. If you are only reading this book as a diversion, or worse, as a parent, consider the sorry state of your existence. Mortgages? Credit Card bills that soar with annual percentage rates compounding at 14.9%? Gingivitis? The painful itch of hemorrhoidal tissues?

Maybe you should consider the life-altering, nerve-shattering, mind-bending metamorphosis to SPONGER. Read on. If you have decided that sponging is not for you, read along as well. Just don't enjoy yourself.

How does one become a sponger?

The first and most important step toward sponging is to **move back home.**

Get there as fast as you can. A parent's home is a sponger's castle. If you never left, great. Stay right where you are, you're already ahead of the game. For those of you who are finding the task difficult, here are a few things to keep in mind when making the big leap.

If your parents are **divorced**, move in with the one who received the best settlement, is least seen and has a crushed-ice maker in the door of the fridge.

If your parents are **no longer with us** (e.g. pushing up daisies or pushing shuffle board disks in a tropical setting), collect as much money as possible and move in with the relative who has the best spare room with a big screen t.v. We have found that grandparents are the most willing to part with spare rooms, often not knowing what they were there for in the first place.

If your parents are still **happily married**, but your room has been converted into a sewing/fitness-room/library, invest in a firm roll-away bed or futon and offer to pull up a piece of floor. Complaining a lot about your back may prove fruitful, but either way remember: home is a womb with a view and it meets all of life's other needs. (Also, though it may take an initial capital investment, the attic option worked well for Greg Brady.)

If your parents are **unhappily married** and still in the same house, you have it made. Call some friends. Print up invitations. You can play one parent against the other every night of your life and reap huge rewards. "No Mom, of course I won't tell Dad about your afternoon shower partner. And oh, by the way, do you have fifty bucks I could borrow?"

So now that you're set up in Sponge Central, you've got it made. Now get over your bad-ass self—that was the easy part. It's time to begin your first **day in the life of a sponger**.

WAKE UP.

The sounds that could possibly awaken you from blissful sleep:

* Your parents' alarm clock.

* The knock of a housekeeper.

* A friend or relative saying it's time to get off the couch.

* The sound of yourself vomiting.

* The mindless chatter of a weatherman on the t.v. that was left on all night.

* The melodic rat-a-tat-tat of an AK-47.

* The Cock-a-doodle-doo of a young rooster bringing
  in the dawn.
  (NOTE: If this is the sound that awakens you, put this book down and run
  for your life. You live on a farm.)

* The wheeze of an insect expiring from the poisonous
  vapors emanating from your mouth.

* The playful banter of self-satisfied
  sanitation engineers disposing of
  your ecology-destroying refuse.

* The soft purr of a jumbo-jet
  engine plummeting to the ground.

* The chime of the campus bell tower.
  (NOTE: If this pertains to you, go back to sleep. You're
  in school and have nothing to worry about... yet.)

* The joyful cackling of school children
  skipping and waving lunch pails in oblivious celebration
  of a worry-free time of life.

* The little voice in your head screaming:
  "Failure! Failure! You're amounting to nothing!"

Close your eyes, and try desperately to reattain dream state.

The sound of your alarm finally invades your skull, waking you.

SMACK
SNOOZE BUTTON.

SMACK
SNOOZE BUTTON.

SMACK
SNOOZE BUTTON.

Blank page to be used to wipe drool off pillow.

Actually take your body out of a reclining position.

GET UP.

HIT THE SHOWERS.

Of course, this depends on where you fell asleep.
If you failed to make it back to Sponge Central,
your bathing options may include:

* A fresh water lake.

* The Y.

* A backyard hose or pool.

* A dog bowl.

* A wet-nap.

* A handy bottle of cologne.

> (WARNING: Last option not recommended for more than seven days as skin
> rashes are expensive to cure. French nationals are, of course, exempt.)

While a dog bowl does have its own unique allure, nothing
quite beats a nice, long shower at home. A lot can be
accomplished under hot water. Which brings us to:

SPONGING PRINCIPLE NUMBER TWO

Always plan a dual purpose for every mundane task.

Here are just a few of the many **practical tasks** you can accomplish in the shower:

* Steam clean wrinkled clothing.

* Transcendentally meditate.

* Listen to morning talk radio and collect exciting facts for use as conversation filler later in the day.

* Conduct self-examinations and save on potential drain to health care system.

* Run scalding water and eradicate bad habits with a funky brand of shock therapy.

* Create body-lint animal sculptures for future gift giving needs.

* Do dishes and earn bonus points with mom.

* Rewire family electrical items.

* Fog up the room, pretend you're at the country club and boss around an imaginary, underpaid staff.

* Enjoy free entertainment, aka: play with self.

GET DRESSED.

While slipping on your well-worn black sneakers, your mind begins to drift. Reel it back in and commence creative daydreaming:

SPONGING PRINCIPLE NUMBER THREE

Always, always daydream with a higher purpose.

DAYDREAM.

Acceptable topics for your first daydream of the day include:

* Plans for an extensive excursion to hubs of European vitality: Florence, Prague, Berlin, Fresno.

* Images of Elle McPherson/David Hasselhoff...or both...or both and a pack of wild dogs...or both and a pack of wild dogs with Sigmund Freud riding bareback on a Shetland pony firing darts into their naked behinds.

* A place on the New York Times bestseller list for your brilliant twenty-something how-to book.

* Rock 'n' roll stardom.

* Your own info-mercial starring LaToya Jackson.

* A career in politics.
  (The politician is the Four Star General of spongers.)

* Ruler of the Universe.

* Joining forces with The Mighty Morphin Power Rangers.

* "I'd like to thank the Academy..."

25

FORAGE FOR BREAKFAST.

As with every hunting and gathering endeavor, creativity is key. Consider the following options:

✴ Raid your parents' cupboard.

✴ Doggy Bag dive in your parents' refrigerator.

✴ Go to a friend or relative's office and, while enjoying free coffee, find company refrigerator and sample other employee's lunches.

✴ Visit any police station and:

- File a fake complaint and get a free donut and a cup of coffee.
- Feign amnesia and get donut and coffee.
- Offer to sell police charity tickets and get donut and coffee.
- Pretend to be an officer and get a dozen donuts and a liter of coffee.

* Chomp a pack of Dexatrim gum.

* Pick and eat fruit from a neighbor's tree.

* Visit your local deli or bakery and, while acting like a finicky customer, get free tastes of as much food as possible.

* Don a Hawaiian shirt, shorts and dress socks, then go to a hotel and indulge yourself in a complimentary continental breakfast.

* Six to eight Flintstones Chewables.

* Casually stroll through a diner and pick morsels off abandoned plates.

* Bum a smoke and a tall glass of water. This should fill you 'til lunch.

* Watch any John Hughes movie. Obsess about the lack of reality. Feel misunderstood. As with Dexatrim, your stomach will be in knots all morning.

* Jog a few miles. The adrenaline should mix with residual alcohol in your blood stream causing a lengthy bout of nausea.

   (NOTE: Rumor has it that this activity is called 'exercise' and actually increases your chance for a long, healthy life. This does not, however, represent the opinions of the authors of this book. It's only mentioned as a prevailing attitude at this time in our nation's history.)

* Skip breakfast entirely, it's overrated.

MAKE MONEY.

Your tummy is warmed with valuable nutrients. It's now time to investigate a few money-making opportunities. A good game plan is crucial for your continual pursuit of higher living. Options include the following schemes...
(NOTE: For dire financial situations, consult Appendix F.)

* Collect aluminum cans. Recycle. Feel the joys of being eco-correct.

* File and collect unemployment benefits.
  (Unfortunately, in most states you'll have to have held down a job for six months to collect.)

* Seek "extra" or "stand-in" work in film, television or commercials. The day wages are low, but quite often, union rules mandate that they feed you.

SPONGING PRINCIPLE NUMBER FOUR
Part-time gigs should always include food.

* Earn "Free Money" for your: blood, sperm/ovum, hair, fingernails. Consult local newspapers for listings.

* Investigate the lucrative field of psychological and physiological experimentation now that testing on lab animals has fallen out of chic. Consult your local college or the Department of Energy.

* Nude model for figure drawing classes. The potential for other contacts is great.
  (NOTE: Check your equipment first to avoid unnecessary humiliation.)

* Gamble.

* Play the stock market with Grandma's money. It's a lot like gambling but sounds better at cocktail parties.

* Delve into a friend's trust fund.

* Start micro-brewing beer out of your home.

* Create your own charitable organization and throw a debutante ball. Reap the rewards of over-zealous mothers desperate to gain acceptance in high society.

* Become a performance artist. Remember no real talent is needed, though a good, deep hat doesn't hurt. This is best accomplished at lunch hour in a busy section of town. "Art" can be anything from screaming obscenities at passersby to sitting still in front of a sign that reads, "human statue."

* Act like a "sidewalk cartoonist," simply draw a stick figure and a well placed symbol of your subject's hobby—such as sex or sports. (Balls are easy to render.)

* Take a Greyhound to Los Angeles, try-out for a game show and win fabulous prizes.

* If all else fails, try to obtain a loan. The following is a partial list of viable lending institutions:

29

VIABLE LENDING

Charitable Organization	Advantages
Grandparents (odds 5:7)	Debts are easily forgotten
Loan Shark (odds 2:1)	Cash on demand
Parents (odds 2 against 1)	None
Student Loan (odds 5:1)	Four years of mindless debauchery
National Endowment for the Arts Grant (odds 120:1)	Potential for project on naked yam dancing
Lottery (odds 120,000,000:1)	"And the schools win too!"

INSTITUTIONS.

Drawbacks

Very poor ratio between amount of cash and amount of cheek squeezing

All those troublesome little fractures

Loss of pride, motivation and couch space

Thirty years of mindful repayment

Potential for project's disposal at last minute by right-wing, Congressional pedophile

Appearance of long lost relatives

PANIC.

A person you knew from your past approaches. Damp with perspiration, you realize that your self-esteem, your inner determination, your raison d'etre is about to be called to task by such painfully competitive questions as, "So how's it going?" A former romantic interest will exacerbate this situation ten-fold.

Unlike your parents, a casual acquaintance never knows if you're lying. Remember, it is crucial to make him or her feel as inferior as possible.

Sample comeback lines include:

* "Going? It's going fine if you like money...
  and lots of it."

* "I guess you didn't hear about my accident?"

* "And your name was what again?"

* "Great. I put together a group of investors. We're
  going to open a small publishing company."

* "Well, with those guest spots on The Simpsons,
  I haven't had much time of late."

* "So, obviously you've met Sy Sperling."

* "I guess one of us hasn't been worried about
  their cholesterol."

* "Sorry, can't chat. I'm late for my Mensa meeting."

* "Is that a Pez dispenser in your pants, or are you just
  happy to see me?"

* "Don't you owe me money?"

* "How many sweet, young animals had to die for
  that briefcase?"

* "Out of my way. I'm on the information superhighway
  and I can't slow down."

TAKE A BREAK.

Time spent making money and coping with anxiety should, of course, be counter-balanced with a fair smattering of fun. Here are some early afternoon entertainment choices:

* Browse at trendy, outdoor newsstands.

* Have a listening party at a local record store.

* Take a library fun tour.
  (NOTE: The authors have no idea what this means, but someone's mother suggested it.)

* Explore seasonal
  park activities:
  • kite flying
  • snowball throwing
  • leaf stomping
  • crack dealer dodging
  • dog petting

* Start a protest. Get a
  following and collect donations.
  You can speak out about anything.
  Megaphones can be made from those empty toilet paper rolls that have been collecting on the bathroom floor.

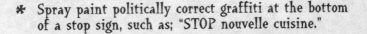

* Spray paint politically correct graffiti at the bottom of a stop sign, such as; "STOP nouvelle cuisine."

* Give a motivational talk during a junior high school lunch period. Sample topic: "This is your lunch on drugs." (See Sponging Principles #2 & #4)

* Do the Hustle.

* Do the Hustle naked.

* Test drive the latest sportscar by driving it to Vegas. Have salesman pay for a Seigfried and Roy matinee in exchange for a safe return.

* Journey into a department store fragrance section and, with the readily available tester bottles, pretend to be one of those annoying beautician/gunslingers.

* Organize a wheelchair derby at the local hospital. Remember to stress that wagering is an effective, time-tested therapy.

* Put on a one-act play in front of security cameras at the neighborhood bank.
  (NOTE: Be sure to write a glamorous part for a humorless guard.)

* Wait in line at a crowded butcher shop, indiscriminantly scream: "Sweet Jesus, the tongue's moving."

Have a random person call your parents' answering
machine and leave a message of gratitude for "coming
in for an interview." Repeat once a week. Consult
doctor or pharmacist if skin irritation occurs.

SCAVENGE FOR LUNCH.

Fingernails are a tasty treat, but they grow so slowly. That, of course, is why we have toenails. But even the hardiest sponger can not subsist on God's little culinary gifts alone. This is where lunch comes in. More than a bothersome biological necessity, it is a welcome respite from the sheer physical effort required to hold your body in a vertical position.

Once again, creativity is key:

* Hit fast food fixin's bars.

* Graze at an understaffed, neighborhood supermarket.

* Crash an office lunch meeting. If questioned, distractedly mutter the words "intern," "first meeting" and "million dollar harassment lawsuit."

* Visit a retirement home, hug a random old person and exclaim: "Hello grandpa. It's so good to see you again." Enjoy a starch-filled feast and tales of The Depression.

* Present a restaurant server with a bogus business card identifying you as a food critic from a little known magazine. Start scribbling angrily into a notepad if you receive a bill.

* Become an international supermodel—photo-shoots are catered. (See Sponging Principle #4.)

* Feast on a nice piece of humble pie.

* Stand by a hot dog cart and wait for rejected misorders. The line, "Is that maggot supposed to be in there?", may facilitate things.

* Bring a box of cookies into a grade school and trade-up for more nutritious items.

* Remember, you're never too old to say "trick-or-treat."

* Use a friend's expense account.

* Flash conscientious restaurant owner a phony badge from the Department of Public Health. If executed confidently, you can sample everything in the kitchen. You may even leave with a doggy bag full of cash.

* Pigeon.

* Keep sleeping. You missed breakfast, why stop now?

While digesting lunch, your mind gears will come to a grinding halt. Do a handstand and begin to daydream.
(See Sponging Principle #3.)

OPPORTUNITIES FOR TRAVEL.

Fantasize. Visualize. Strategize. Dematerialize. Getting out once in a while is neat, so use this time to ponder the easy means to sponging your way anywhere and everywhere...

* Form a successful pop band and tour distant lands.

* Become a freight car hobo.

* Find someone looking to have their car driven across country. This possibility actually exists. Check your local paper.

* House-sit for someone who lives by the zoo and pretend you're on a safari.

* Maim yourself and join the circus as its latest freak.

* Old-fashioned hitch hiking.

* Seek political asylum in a country of your choice.

* Plan a normal trip; have a catastrophe in the snow or desert; eat friends' buttocks in desperate cannibalistic act of survival; sell rights to NBC.

* Get paid to ship "freight" in your luggage space.

* Set up a fundraiser: "Jog for Hypochondria".

* Get sequestered for jury duty. Pays $5 a day and a motel room with a chain-smoking civil servant. If fortunate, case revolves around high profile sports figure and you can sell your tale for six figures.

* Develop a convincing life story and get on a talk show. Airfare and hotels are included. In order to dazzle the segment producers, incorporate at least three of the following elements:
  • nymphomania
  • topless dancing
  • family tree that doesn't fork
  • fear of breathing
  • Gary Coleman

* Peace Corps or Club Med: The Ultimate Quandary. See following page:

PEACE CORPS
A Philosophical

Peace Corps

"The toughest job you'll ever love"

No t.v. or phone

Deal with infuriating political systems laid out by
ego-maniacal leaders

Tan body while hunting for edible food

Plant life-giving trees in freshly plowed soil

Discuss limbo of third world economies

Collect sea shells with neighboring children

Learn a variety of languages

Paramilitary

vs. Club Med

Debate

Club Med

"The antidote to civilization"

No t.v. or phone

Deal with infuriating political systems laid out by ego-maniacal instructors

Hunt for tan bodies after digesting food

Plant lifeless, freshly plowed friends in soil

Discuss limbo competitions

Collect neighboring children with currency shells

Learn a variety of Lambadas

Parasailing

GO HOME.

Take the initiative to switch parents' long distance carrier and earn hundreds of dollars in free long distance minutes. Do a major tap dance on Ma Bell's grave, then wait for an exciting new promotion from another carrier and switch again.

TURN ON TELEVISION.

TV is not a mindless activity—it is a sensible way to make yourself a better human. With this easy-to-follow television curriculum, afternoons spent prostrate on the couch can be as enlightening as years at the most expensive institutions of higher learning.

Cultural Anthropology 1: Nothing explores the cultural landscape better than the "Talk Show." Find out how to better sponge off the fringe elements as well as the mainstream. For example, on Oprah you'll learn that your quiet Uncle Eddie might appreciate a leather harness and a scrotal ring, a gesture that may prove profitable down the road.

Physical Anthropology 1: Explore the darkest reaches of Darwinism and marvel at those abnormal specimens that have not only survived and evolved, but have thrived in the primordial, prime-time world. The "fittest" include Tattoo, Alf, Worf, Screech, Urkel and Larry King.

Calculus 1a: Discover your own theorems based on old sitcoms. Become the Pythagoras of your time. Impress friends and influence people. The "standards" includes the "What's Happening," wherein the height of Shirley's 'fro, divided by the circumference of Rerun's waistline squared, equals the number of times Duane says "Huh?" in your average episode.

Economy 2: "Sesame Street." This is a core requirement enabling all spongers to grasp the basics of monetary exchange. Especially noteworthy are Oscar the Grouch's Machiavellian principles and the Hobbsian-Locke banter between Bert and Ernie. These two are also to be examined in Psychology 134: Homoeroticism in Modern Society. (NOTE: Don't look at Big Bird, it'll just make you hungry.)

Linguistics 10: Learn the etymology of practical vernacular from those in the know—the street hustler, thug, pimp and junkie. From the chronicles of "Dragnet", "Hawaii Five-O", "Starsky and Hutch" and "Hill Street Blues", we can trace the origin of once current lingo and see how it fits into our daily lives and rituals. "Slap me some mondo bread scumbag, or I'll off you with your own piece," is an expression that incorporates almost every decade of the twentieth century. It does *not* translate to "Hit me with an open hand and some large leavened item you used condom, or I'll remove myself from your person with your own part." Tune in and find out what this really means; it's sure to come in handy for the modern sponger in his/her attempts to be oblique.

Paleontology 14: Working or Buried? To balance out a rigorous schedule, this course of study is best utilized during commercials or while channel grazing. Stop quickly on old programming and ask yourself, is a particular actor/actress still working, or are they dead? This is to be taken in the literal sense, you know, acting for the big director in the sky. It can be tricky, for some careers might have turned to dust, but the people themselves are indeed alive and dusting off their 8x10 glossies.

Political Science 1: MTV News.

Psychology 4: "Psychic Friends Network." Study the paranoid, delusional mind at work. It can be an interactive course if you're not paying the phone bills.

Physics 10: Monster Truck rallies and World Wrestling bouts. Both exhibit dualities of Quantum Mechanics: How can things so big move so fast; how can something so asinine bring in so many paying spectators. Potential career opportunities abound.

Sociology 24b: "Cops", "America's Most Wanted" and "Unsolved Mysteries". Learn from the mistakes of mammothly failed spongers.

PANIC.

While flipping channels, you accidentally come across something that makes you insanely jealous:

* Gorgeous, glowing, gallavanting couples that seem to have just experienced the greatest sexual acts known to man.

* A trendy item of clothing you've only seen in a magazine that you couldn't even afford and only read about at your mom's office.

* A vintage car that your father said you'd never be able to afford.

* A jungle of tanned, toned bodies.

In other words, you've just seen a promo for this week's episode of "Baywatch".

Once the angst-driven perspiration evaporates off your sunken brow, you make a commitment to...

WORK ON YOUR IMAGE.

Christopher Lasch once said, "Nothing succeeds like the appearance of success." We don't know who he is either.

We just pilfered the quote from "The Portable Curmudgeon", a handy sponger reference when strong logic is needed.

Point being, in order to sponge your way through your twenties (and beyond), you must appear successful. And as Shakespeare wrote in Hamlet, "the apparel oft proclaims the man." While the sponger is often on the move, out of money and, quite possibly, color blind from lack of protein, he/she can still look the part.

Here are a few **fashion recommendations**. You should possess:

* As much underwear as possible, as there is obviously little time for laundry in a sponger's busy day. Don't forget that every pair has two sides.

* At least one pair of black jeans: Goes well with everything and gets you over anywhere from an art opening to dinner at Chez something.

* A classic black baseball hat for bad hair days, in the right company, makes you look like a hip director/minor league infielder.

* Black tee-shirts: simple, stylish, and hard to stain.

* Black blazer: simple, stylish, and easy to stuff.

* Comfortable black shoes.

SPONGING PRINCIPLE NUMBER FIVE
No shirt, no shoes, no sponging.

Y ou ask yourself, "How am I supposed to get these stylish duds?" Well, consider all the options for procuring the wardrobe you desire, always keeping in mind that even though the wrinkled look comes in and out of vogue, rayon shirts have been known to go as long as two years without cleaning...

BASIC CLOTHING COLLECTING.

* Visit sample sales.

* Make friends with rich people your size.

* Hit a thrift store one-stop: Sell friends' clothes or your own rejects and keep the money. Be sure to sell unwashed clothes and save on laundry expenses.

* Convince your relatives to lose weight. Pick up their obsolete items and sell, wear or trade.

* Get a part-time job at fast food restaurant with a cool uniform.

* Join local clubs and sports teams, get cool logoed shirts and jackets.

* Make a business card proclaiming you as the Rock Journalist in your area, mail to publicists at record labels asking to be on mailing lists. Within six to eight weeks, you'll receive shirts and hats galore, though you might be asked to cover a band and write a lengthy article.

* Change your name to one letter (i.e. 'I' or 'E'), and become a happening high fashion model, take home designer clothes after shoots.
(WARNING: This option may lead to quick dashes to the toilet after meals.)

* When doting relatives call to ask "How are you?", answer subtly, "Everything's great (cough, cough), I'm just a little cold (sneeze). All my clothes have holes in them." Within six to eight days, new apparel arrives.

* Tell your parents that you just missed out on a fabulous job, which would've taken you out of the house, because you didn't have the right threads. Within six to eight hours...

* Run naked through the streets and get arrested. Jailhouse attention might be uncomfortable, but the free clothing is easily sold.

* Join a fanatic, religious cult. (Catholic Monastery/Nunneries are included.) Indulge yourself in the crystalline gestalt of commune wear.

Above space may be utilized by the police sketch artist who renders the image of the guy who stole your father's hubcaps. (see Appendix F)

TESTIMONIAL: "HOLEY JEANS BATMAN."

"I visited my grandparents one Sunday and worked it. I purposely wore a pair of torn Levis, almost bare at both knees, to their house, and, in a matter of milliseconds, they noticed. 'Look at you. Your underwear's showing,' Nana commented in horror. I neglected to tell them that my shredded jeans are comfortable and took upwards of three years to reach their present, highly desirable state. A embarrassed shrugs and noncommittal comments later and we were streaking to the mall. Actually it was more like crawling, and the place we ended up wasn't really a mall. But I got two new pairs of Levis to be worked into the rotation; and my grandparents, well, they got the satisfaction of being sponged, along with the warmth, contentment and inner peace that comes with it."

— Bob B.

"P.S. They also got a couple of excellent hints on how to get back home."

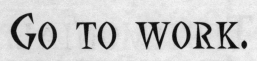

GO TO WORK.

A sponger's official workday begins when parents come home from theirs. It is imperative to be well prepared for this, the most challenging part of your day. Your survival depends on it.

Listen carefully for that nerve wrenching sound of key hitting lock, for you are about to be judged. Stay calm. This handy list of do's and don'ts will get you through.

DO...

Do look busy.

Do have computer on.

Do sit hunched over vocational training books.

Do display grad. school applications across floor.

Do put finishing touches on meal in kitchen.

Do get caught vacuuming and dusting furniture.

Do open door and exclaim, "Welcome home!"

Do hang up coat and serve parent a drink.

Do say, "I've set up several job interviews with very prestigious firms today."

Do blurt out, "It must feel great to come home after a hard day's work."

Do offer to take the family out for a nice meal.

DON'T...

Don't look drunk.

Don't have "Love Connection" on.

Don't sit hunched over mail-order underwear catalogs.

Don't display naked, afternoon sex partner across floor.
(Quickly deflate/unplug and store.)

Don't finish touching self in kitchen.

Don't get caught sleeping and drooling on furniture.

Don't open door and exclaim, "What are you doing here?"

Don't serve personal hang-ups and fix yourself a drink.

Don't say, "I've slept all day, and I'm still tired."

Don't blurt out, "When's dinner ready."

Don't bring wallet if taken up on offer.

PANIC.

Despite your best attempts to deflect attention from your spongosity, parents may still spew one or more of the following panic-inducing pontifications:

* "I just talked to your cousin Louie and he has an opening in the stapling department at his factory."

* "Do you have that twenty grand you owe me?"

* "Are you planning on getting married and raising your family in the basement?"

* "When I was your age...(insert trite anecdote here).

* "As long as you're home, why don't you join us and the Thomasons for a game of pinochle."

* "Get out of my chair."

* "I was just laid off, so we're going to have to tighten our belts around here."

* "Here's a brochure you should look over. I want you to be all that you can be."

* "This is Dr. Sachs. He has a few questions to ask you."

* "Dad and I are moving to Boca Raton, Florida."

* "What smells in here?"

* "I could've sworn that mayonnaise jar was full of pennies."

* "Do you think you can live like this forever?"

PREPARE FOR BATTLE.

Before you get into a heated debate with your parents,
leave and hide in your room. Sometimes, though, a quick
diversion is the only escape. To accomplish this, and thus
insure your sponging future, you will have to be well-versed
in covert manipulation.

The key here is the **exceptionally oblique diversion line**.
Use the following statements as templates—inserting your
own personal information where needed—in order to confuse
the living crap out of your parents.
(HINT: Make sure to work the lines into everyday conversation, while always
remembering the seductive power of food.)

ATTACH YOURSELF TO A GREATER SOCIAL PHENOMENON
"I'm not a lazy parasite. I'm a functioning dichotomy swept
up in the battered remnants of the twentieth century...
Speaking of batter, what do you say to some fishsticks?"

FIND SOLACE IN THE APOCALYPTIC APPROACH
"Why buy into the whole work ethic thing? The planet's
going to explode into flames anyday and all of human history
is going with it... Are you going to finish that sandwich?"

IMPLEMENT THE "WAITING FOR GODOT"
(While pointing to phone) "Any minute now, that puppy's
going to ring and bring me the windfall of a lifetime...
Either that or it's the Domino's guy. Tell him I'm in the shower."

USE THE QUASI-ACADEMIC ANGLE
"I'm studying the post-modern construct of angst from the inside out... Are we still out of Mallomars?"

BE THE TORTURED ARTIST YOU'VE ALWAYS WANTED TO BE
"My soul! My soul!" (Ripping at own flesh, rounds out the concept.) "Chinese anyone?"

ATTACK THE AMERICAN DREAM
"(Insert name of dead relative here) came to this country so that his/her children would have opportunities the old country couldn't provide, and you guys worked real hard so that your children could have the things you never did, and, well, I think it's high time for someone to enjoy all this intensive labor... And a large fries please."

INVOKE AN AWE-INSPIRING EUROPEAN WORLD-VIEW
"C'est la vie... Did I mention *french* fries?"

FEIGN SUDDEN MENTAL ILLNESS
"Happy Birthday Mr. President! (bark) (bark) Until the one day when this lady met this fellow... I can't get enough Halavah."

SIMPLY USE THE WORD 'MULL'
"I'm mulling over a high-powered record and movie deal... Is this hot mulled cider?"

With parents rattled and diverted, bid them a fond goodnight, maybe a hug or a kiss, then bolt out the door before they ask for the car keys. If time permits, make yourself a little snack for the road.

SCROUNGE FOR THE EVENING MEAL.

Consider these fine options:

* You could always eat dinner with your parents. This is dangerous, as there's lots of time for scrutiny and questions about your existence.

* If lucky, your parents will visit a friend's house for dinner, leaving the kitchen to yourself. Healthy tips include:
  • Breakfast cereals are not just for breakfast; you get 8 essential vitamins and minerals.
  • Toast and Tang; if the astronauts did it, hey.

* Go to a Gallery opening. Though pretentiousness may divert your appetite, a fist full of biscuits and overly ripe cheese can go an awfully long way.

* Throw a pot-luck supper. This nets dinner and left-overs for weeks, plus it doubles mom's tupperware collection. You only have to make the phone calls.

* At sporting events, sit towards the middle of a long row and commandeer food being passed from vendors down the aisle. Distract rightful recipient with a clever line like, "Hey isn't that Gary Coleman?"

* Don't eat dinner, live off body-fat.

* Enjoy free vegetarian meals at the Hare Krishna complex.
  (WARNING: If you wake up in the morning dressed in a pink sheet,
  you've become a member of a cult. Don't Panic! You have joined the ranks of
  one of the world's finest professional sponging operations. Congratulations.)

* Visit nearest resort location and sign meals to
  Jay Blumenfield in room #401.
  (NOTE: The two authors who actually proof-read this book are not
  responsible for any damages that may result.)

* Try our Famous Condiment Soup Recipe: 4 packets
  tomato ketchup, 1/2 packet mustard, 2 scoops relish,
  2 tubes salt, 5 tubes of pepper, mayonnaise to taste.

* Show up at friend's after mealtime
  and clean off scraps under the
  guise of helping do the dishes.

* Of course, there's also The Fine
  Art of Restaurant Dining:
  • Happy-hour foods:
    "The Beauty of Pretzels".
  • Doctor your driver's license
    for free birthday meals.
  • Utilize a "2" fer "1" dinner special with a friend buying the "1".
  • Hit up out-of-town relatives, or friends' relatives,
    for expensive meal. (Remember, visitors are more
    generous in the early days of their stay.)

* Dine out alone, but bring along an assortment of
  insects for tasteful placement in ordered dishes.
  (See following page for proper placement technique.)

Entomological Culinary Suggestions

While a common housefly goes quite well with most soups and salads, main courses often require a heartier/leggier choice. For light pasta dishes, we suggest any member of the arachnid family, while heavier meat dishes may require a more full-bodied selection. Winged insects nicely complement most cream sauces.

When notifying your server of the "uninvited dinner guest" at your table, look appropriately disturbed and wait for the manager to suggest a free meal. If only a complementary wine or dessert is offered, drop first name of local food critic between convincing bouts of dry heaving. An extra bug wing or leg between your front teeth should clinch the deal.

TESTIMONIAL: "MY DINNER WITH ANDREA."

"I love gambling. Risks sometime backfire, but this time it came up sevens. I had invited myself, along with a friend in from out of town, to a dinner with a moderately high powered business woman he had slept with five years prior. We decided on an upscale Italian restaurant where salads often make it to double digits. I was feeling lucky. I ordered a bottle of wine, an appetizer and an entree. I was feeling lucky. I ordered an espresso and chocolate tart. I was feeling lucky. The check arrived and I casually leaned to the woman, with eyes crossed in drunkenness, and said, 'Please thank your company for me. This meal was excellent.' Not wanting to seem ungracious, she whipped out the company credit card and I leaned back, ordering another coffee drink and a rack of lamb to go. All the while, I was relishing the fact that I didn't have to be at the office by 9:00."

— Charles P.

TAKE OFF.

At long last, the moon has taken hold of the sky. For the non-sponging population, nighttime represents complete leisure time. Yet, for the sponger it is anything but. There are just too many opportunities to pass up.

SPONGING PRINCIPLE NUMBER SIX

The more people you meet, the more stuff you can sponge.

Watch "Wheel of Fortune" in an electronics store. This is simply a warm-up stretch for the mind. Gear up for the evening's strenuous situations by joining Pat and Vanna in Surround Sound on twenty-four state-of-the-art screens.

T	H	R	□	□	□	N	C	□
W	A	S	A
M	A	N	□	R	□	M
N	A	N	T	□	C	□	□	T

LIVE IT UP.

The following is a list of some cost-efficient, early evening activities. It's still early, so you should make a valiant effort to spend as little money as possible. Maybe you can even obtain some extra pocket change.

* Continue watching television.

* Equip yourself with cocktail party banter by brushing up on the beginnings or endings of all the latest feature film releases at your local megaplex.

* Visit a pool hall and hustle money.
(NOTE: Real knowledge and ability are required.)

* For extra fun, ask the guy at the next table if he has fifteen balls, then when he nods his head yes, laugh and say, "Oh my God, you can sire your own country."

* Visit local video arcade. Hover over kids, wink and say, "I love watching how you move." Ask for money to leave.

* Go to the office of a late-working friend. Use phone, finish off coffee pots and photocopy body parts to get a head start on holiday card rush.

* Snooze on Craftmatic adjustable bed with lumbar support until department store closes.

* Go to a Greek restaurant and release a bit of tension by breaking a few plates and downing a few shots of Ouzo. Pretend to be tardy relative. Add "opadopolous" to your last name.

* Push on closed eyelids and marvel at the wacky optical laser show.

* Go door-to-door trying to register voters. Wrestle with the blatant ignorance of your neighbors.

* Recruit a friend's younger sibling. Go to any local concert in town. Force the child to beg for extra tickets using such gems as, "I hate it when Uncle Herbie leaves me outside to watch his car all night," or "Excuse me, madam? Have you heard of The Make A Wish Foundation?" Turn around and scalp "donated" seats for generous profit.

Blank page to be used to wipe off finger-printing ink.

PANIC.

Watching your friend's younger sibling try to find his way back to a part of town he vaguely recognizes, you begin to think back to your own innocent childhood when sponging was a much easier way of life. A sense of dread grips your heart.

You grope at your expanding buttocks. You feel the weight of your face beginning to droop as gravity pulls your body and soul into an abyss of regret.

What you are currently experiencing is an existential crisis of epic proportions. Your cerebral cortex is grid-locked. An overly accelerated heart rate depletes your system of calming oxygen and the rapidly firing synapses of your nerve endings explode with destructive power.

Ignore.

BAR HOP.

Visit various local watering holes where spongers' delights should be in obvious abundance. With sufficiently baggy clothing you can go home with anything from paper goods and kitchen utensils to little umbrellas and nicely broken-in cigarettes. For our intellectually challenged spongers, we recommend against taking ice.

And if you know where to look, you can save your parents bushels of money on therapy. Bar denizens are usually quite chatty and have a wealth of experience to share.

Consult the following symptom list to locate the appropriate therapist nearest you:

If you feel you're suffering from an **Oedipal Complex**: Seek out a Hell's Angel with "MOM" tattooed on his hairy, beefy biceps.

If a **paranoia attack** occurs, find:
The drunkest person around and tell him that an FBI transmitter is sticking out of the back of his neck.

If you're feeling **anti-social**:
Talk to the little person inside your head.

If you are afflicted with **delusions of grandeur**:
Talk to God.

If you simply feel **depressed**:
Order another drink.

If you think you're being **persecuted**:
Discuss the issue of gays in the military with a member of the Armed forces.

And whatever these people say...
do the exact opposite.

KEEP HOPPING.

You'll know it's time to leave the bar when:

* You've just heard yourself say, "Drinks for everyone, on me."

* You accidentally notice an old woman carving her name into your stomach with a shrimp fork.

* You've just volunteered to clean.

* During a rerun of "I Love Lucy" on the big screen, you weep openly.

* You find yourself sampling the nuts and vegetables on the bar stools instead of the bar trays.

* The massive weight of "borrowed" items pops a button on your shirt.

* You find yourself attracted to the soda dispenser.

* You notice that the image of a headless chicken happens to be tattooed on *your* forearm.

* You consider licking the neon signs in the windows.

* You smell like urine.

* You start writing poetry on a cocktail napkin.

* You start reciting that poetry in the restroom.

* You actually think the person sitting next to you *is* Gary Coleman.

* You find yourself solving the health care crisis.

* You hear about a happening party that's just a few minutes away!

TESTIMONIAL: "MARTINIS, STOCK TIPS AND LEOTARDS."

"I never met a drunk guy I didn't like. I mean, it's so easy to refill their glass with water after downing the beverage yourself. You don't even have to pull that, 'Hey, isn't that...' trick. Or even the more degrading, 'Hi, my name's Alexandra. Will you buy me a drink?' I don't go in for that sexist crap. The best part, though, is all the cool information you can learn from men who've thrown back a few. Once this guy told me where he invested his money and I gave my father a great insider-stock tip the next morning as I ate the last frozen waffle.

Another time I learned about this health club where all the employees are invited in for major deli-platters on the last Friday of the month. What was one more girl in a leotard?"

-Alexandra J.

CRASH A PARTY.

If the front door is not wide open, a perfectly honed entrance line might be necessary. Regardless of your sex, it never hurts to show a little flesh.

There are only two lines you need remember. "Excuse me, but have you met my friend George Washington?", is basically a master key. Otherwise, stand up tall and utter, "Let me in, damnit." Resist the urge to introduce Andrew Jackson. Even if the party sounds amazing, there's usually a back door.

Much like an elaborate miniature golf course, parties are filled with both moving and stationary obstacles. The real secret to successfully navigating the course is simple. Just view Partygoers as those seductive, astro-turf putting greens, each with its own narrow ramp to great position and its hidden passages to complete dead ends.

Creating a meaningful friendship is nice and all, but, in the attempt to be the fittest of spongers, remember that only the most absorbent survive.

THE NINE HOLES
OF FRIENDSHIP.

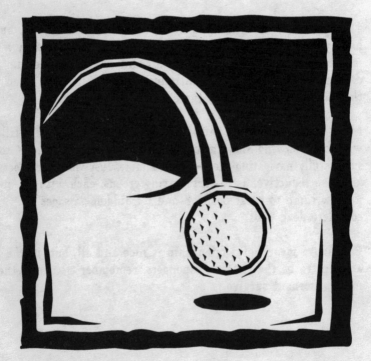

1 **The Food Service Employee:** Tell-tale signs are a "May I help you" button, mustard stains, or residue of fried animal products. Tends to hang out near the food table re-organizing the garnish. At fancier shindigs, will be carrying a tray.

If played *correctly*:
Your fridge is always stocked with others' leftovers and drawers are filled with ketchup packets for our "Famous Condiment Soup" recipes.
If played *poorly*:
Acne may result.

2 **The Mouse Potato:** This computer geek is recognizable by his or her incessant use of acronyms that you've never heard.

If played *correctly*:
You can gain access to the information super-highway and the joys of international cyber-sponging. At the very least, you can pull off free movie channels and long distance calls.
If played *poorly*:
This walking quicksand trap will make you mega-bored talking about mega-bytes.

3 **The Fashionable Person Your Size:** Easily recognized.

If played *correctly*:
Say goodbye to outmoded familial hand-me-downs.
If played *poorly*:
Annoying, anatomical twin may take a shine to your ripped, black ensemble.

The Mortuary Attendant: Recognizable by an overwhelming scent of formaldehyde and an unsettling grin.

If played *correctly*:
Access to free flower arrangements and the latest in facial cosmetics.
If played *poorly*:
Find yourself in a long line for tickets to a Cure concert.

The Valet Parking Attendant: The red vest and lead foot make him an obvious target.

If played *correctly*:
Access to amazing automobiles for "time share."
If played *poorly*:
You'll be constantly hit up for tips.

The Worker Bee (Salon/Record Store/Copy Store/Jewelry Store/Clothing Store Employee): Recognizable by firm handshake and perpetually flowing mindless chatter. Head tilt and unique aroma will vary.

If played *correctly*:
Access to cuts, polishes, discs, and liquid paper, not to mention phenomenally valuable discounts.
If played *poorly*:
Baldness, deafness, paper cuts, metal poisoning, and skin rashes.

7

The Celebrity Brat: Shows an uncanny resemblance to a famous parent or a wanton disregard for human life.

If played *correctly*:
Tropical vacations, gala events, elaborate gifts.
If played *poorly*:
Tropical vacations, gala events, elaborate gifts.

8

The Handicapped Person: Listing characteristics would be in poor taste.

If played *correctly*:
The best parking spots in town.
If played *poorly*:
Exploitation of the physically challenged dooms your immortal soul to Hell for eternity.

9

The Office Slug: Recognizable by unique pallor caused by an eternity spent under fluorescent lighting.

If played *correctly*:
Can provide a cover for occasions when it's advantageous to convince your parents that you are being productive and "have just stepped away from your desk."
If played *poorly*:
Your parents, under the mistaken impression that you actually have an income, may insist that you fork over some cash for rent.
(Remember to always use the word: "Internship.")

REFUEL AT A LOCAL COFFEE HOUSE.

The late night coffee shop is the **Spongers Black Market.** For the low admission price of a bottomless cup of java, sponger's of all shapes and sizes, colors and creeds, convene on ripped leatherette to trade the bits and pieces of mainstream society that have been sponged during the course of their day. This is where all efforts come to fruition.

Here are but two of the possible scenarios going down at diners across this great land. (Check your sponging aptitude here.)

Scenario #1:

Mary, 22, has two tickets to the Chiefs game that her little cousin scrounged up in front of Arrowhead Stadium. She vetoes a trade with Mike, 25, for a weekend at his parents' cabin by the lake in order to utilize Katie's Gap employee discount to purchase the denim shirt that Guy, 23, knows his older sister has been wanting for months. Through this exchange, Guy gets his sister's passionate plea to their parents, "Don't worry, I really think he'll come around soon. All he needs is a few extra bucks."

The Analysis:

Should Mary have taken the enticing weekend at the lake-side cabin? Is Mary just a caring and generous person? No and no! Mary is an all-star sponger. Her exceptional networking and strategizing skills will get her four bottles of her father's favorite Zinfandel because Guy's sister's boyfriend works a catering job which nets quite a chest of spoils. Mary's father is so excited by her generous offering that he overlooks the phone bill and small fender bender she incurred two nights prior. Thus, Mary insures her peaceful existence for at least another couple of months.

Scenario #2:

Dustin, 21, hooks up with Zoe, also 21, who has a connection with a mortician's son. Dustin gets himself the pick of the floral arrangement bonanza from the boom in business following an eighteen car pile-up just outside of town. Dustin decides to use his flowers to woe Angelique, 17, a knock-out who works at a record store on weekends.

The Analysis:

Is this a worthwhile deal? The answer is a resounding, "No Way!" Not only does Angelique lack the most important asset of any potential date, her own apartment, but her job at the record store only entitles her to give early admission to record signing events, the last of which was Kenny G. Had Dustin pushed himself a little further, he would have noticed the dirt under the fingernails of Steve, 27. A few pointed questions and Dustin would have learned some crucial information: Steve's a "fix-it guy" who needed the finishing touches for his mother's birthday dinner. With his flowers, Dustin would have gained access to the hotly desired, or easily tradable, movie channel unscrambling. Free HBO and Showtime can do wonders for chronically irascible parental units.

HEAD HOME.

Having exhausted all trading possibilities, grudgingly point yourself towards Sponge Central.

If, perchance, you feel it might be time to spend a night away from home—like maybe your parents changed the locks, or tearfully screamed into the night, "I have no child"—then, consider these options:

* Ride public transportation 'til dawn.

* Kick out a neighbors' feeble dog from cozy wooden nook.

* Play family members against each other, "Sorry Grandma, but Mom and Dad are into that ritual sacrifice thing again."

* Run around yelling and get institutionalized.

* Camp out in a sporting goods store. Bonfires are generally discouraged but are rarely stopped by the overhead sprinklers before the marshmallows are nice and toasty.

* Consider... **Dating.**

The most important requirement for maintaining a successful sponging relationship is that your chosen partner inhabits a space big enough for two. If that's the case, then the following list of subtle questions will allow you to discover if that person has those other truly endearing qualities:

* "How do you get here often?" (working auto)

* "What's your street sign?" (social status/potential for satellite dish)

* "What's a nice girl/guy like you doing in a bank like this?" (healthy checking account balance)

(NOTE: Due to the unfortunate, yet continuing, patriarchal nature of society, dating is recommended for women spongers only. Male spongers should proceed at their own damn risk.)

CRAWL TO BED.

Congratulations, you have sponged your way through an entire day. You have achieved something great. You are a remarkable human being. In the distant future, mankind will look back on your success with admiration. Well, either that or a great deal of ridicule.

SPONGING PRINCIPLE NUMBER SEVEN

Never go to sleep angry, never go to sleep scared, never go to sleep worrying more about tomorrow than you did about today.

As you drift off to sleep, try and ponder one or more of life's larger questions...

Dream: The Final Frontier

* "Why are you here?"

* "Is there a god?"

* "Potatoes or stuffing?"

* "What if there were no hypothetical questions?"

* "If a tree falls in the woods and nobody is there to hear it, will your father still blame you?"

* "What's the sound of one hand clapping?"

* "What's the sound of one-thousand hands clapping? And don't you wish you knew?"

* "Why does the person who snores the loudest always fall asleep first?"

* "Which came first: The McNugget or the McRib?"

* "Could God make a rock band so big, even he couldn't lift it?"

* "If the world was color blind, how would anyone know when the light turned green?"

* "If Einstein was so smart, why's he dead?"

Free toilet paper.

WAKE UP.

The sounds that could possibly awaken you from blissful sleep...

GLOSSARY OF TERMS.

Ajax (noun): A sponger's best friend.

ATM (noun): Father. Usage: "Oh no, I think the ATM's broke. I won't be able to pay for the movies tonight."

Attend class (verb): Watch television.

Biosphere (noun): Self-contained office building filled with food and supplies. Usage: "I'm going over to my dad's biosphere to use the phone and grab some crackers."

Bonaduce (noun): Someone who's been sponging for over two decades.

Gary Coleman (person): Thespian, born February 8, 1968 in Zion, IL. Starred in the hit sitcom "Diff'rent Strokes."

Collect-call (verb): To get someone else to pay for something. Usage: "I just collect-called this steak to my friend's expense account."

Dalai Lama (noun): The best sponger in the neighborhood.

Dishwasher (noun): Mother. Usage: "Oh no, I think the dishwasher's broke. I won't be able to pay for the movies tonight."

Double-dip (verb): To sponge off another sponger.

Effort-impaired-need-minded-receiver (noun): A politically correct sponger.

E.T. (verb): To get money wired from home.

Fungus (noun): A mettlesome younger sibling.

Kitchen Sink (noun): Sponge Central, home base, the 'rents'.

Last hurrah (noun): Meal with grandparents or anybody leaving town.

Lazy: (No definition available).

Loofa (noun): A sponger from abroad.

Marla (verb): To make a big score.

Moldy (adjective): Fluish; under the weather; not up to sponging.

Oil spill (noun): A visit from rich relatives (In extreme cases, **Exxon Valdez** is used to denote a visit from a rich, terminally-ill relative with no direct heirs).

Pre-sponger (noun): Sponger with acne.

Proto-sponger (noun): Sponger with diaper rash.

Professor (noun): T.V. set.

Reef (noun): Sponger's bedroom.

Sinead (verb): To have a great situation and blow it.

Soap on a rope (noun): A depressed/suicidal person.

Sponge bath (noun): A blatant mistruth. Usage: "Canning fish in Alaska was a complete sponge bath. I had to work my ass off."

Ten-thirteen (noun): Sponger in need of assistance.

Wang Chung (noun): A former all-star sponger who has lost the touch.

Jesse White (noun/person): Mother's therapist/commercial actor who plays the Maytag repairman.

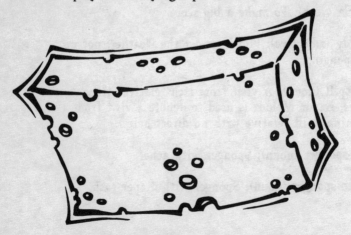

VALUABLE SKILLS AND INVESTMENTS.

* A Second-hand **tuxedo/formal dress:** Two words...
Wedding Buffet.

* Ability to **cook:** Invite friends over and use parents
food. Collect wine to give as gifts to parents over
following weeks. "What a nice surprise dear!"

* **Preset phones:** Use for radio call-ins which can net
tickets and goods for resale or trade.

* A **t.v. set** for the family dining area: You can always
find something noteworthy on the tube to deflect
attention from yourself.

* A **fake identification:** Proving yourself to be under 14,
or over 65, will allow you to eat and see movies for
close to half price.

* A **date book:** Filled with companies and agencies
you've "been actively pursuing."

THE PARENTAL SAVERS INDEX.

SAMPLE BUSINESS CARD.

The Food Critic, The Music Journalist, etc.

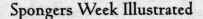

Spongers Week Illustrated

YOUR NAME
Your made up position

Your address
Your phone number
Your Internet number
Your liquor license number

THE SPONGING PRINCIPLES.

Sponging Principle Number One
Work output should never equal or, God forbid, exceed the volume of benefits gained. In other words, **"Life's short, work little."**

Sponging Principle Number Two
Always plan a dual purpose for every mundane task.

Sponging Principle Number Three
Always, always daydream with a higher purpose.

Sponging Principle Number Four
Part-time gigs should always include food.

Sponging Principle Number Five
No shirt, no shoes, no sponging.

Sponging Principle Number Six
The more people you meet, the more stuff you can sponge.

Sponging Principle Number Seven
Never go to sleep scared, never go to sleep angry, never go to sleep worrying more about tomorrow than you did about today.

Bonus Sponging Principle (Not Available On Cassette Version)
Goodnight. Thanks for coming. Drive safely. Be good to each other.

GREAT SPONGERS THROUGH TIME.

Throughout the millennia, there have been a select band of intellectual renegades—the Robin Hoods of thought—who have contributed to the proud legacy of the human race and set the standards for the spongers of today. Some of these little known masters are here recognized:

Jane of Arc: Little known martyr's assistant who used the notoriety of the more famous Joan to sell souvenirs such as "My parents went to a burning at the stake and all I got was this lousy t-shirt" at the local town square.

Billy Bonaparte: Sampled the best French cuisine in the world by convincing his Uncle Napoleon that a secret plot to poison him was abrew. Billy, the official food taster, died an untimely death in a run-in with the official cutlery sharpener, Sheri Bonaparte-Stein.

Morty Columbus: Got to sail the seven seas for free after deciding to keep younger step-brother Christopher's secret, an addiction to Dramamine, to himself.

Tammi Davis Jr.: Florida resident who, in 1973, converted to Judaism and had one eyed surgically removed in exchange for an Olga Korbet dollhouse. To this day, a quick three song set still commands a free dinner buffet, a sauna and a rub-down in retirement communities across the state.

Jerry Descartes: Rene's younger brother, whose pearl "I sleep, therefore I am," transformed Somnambulism forever.

Eve: First Woman, and only known person to have sponged a bone from a man and not had to give anything in return.

Jerry Van Winkle: Rip's second cousin on his father's side, whose forward thinking netted him 20 years of rent-free lodging and mutton burgers. Rumor had it that Mrs. Van Winkle was not actually dead when Rip awoke, but was shacked up with Jerry somewhere in the Detroit area.

Shemp Wright: The third of the famed flying Wright brothers, who earned the first frequent flyer upgrade on Kitty Hawk when he decided against suing Orville over the rights to the "honey roasted" nut.

EMERGENCY SPONGING TECHNIQUES.

The following are to be used only as a last resort and should be used sparingly. If these are overused, the fallout created could dry out your welcome at Sponge Central.

* Offer to run errands for parents. Lose the receipts and keep the change.

* Siphon out the cheap gasoline that dad uses and sell to friends as high octane.

* Get engaged and have a really big party thrown for you. Wake up. Sell gifts. If booty is not sufficient, get married. Repeat.

* Sell dad's hubcaps and say they were swiped while you were interviewing for a job.

* Go to local Victoria Secret store and pick up a dozen lingerie catalogues. Then, proceed to grade school and auction off to highest bidders.

* Get hit by a city bus and survive. (Free ice cream cups and jello, a t.v. over your bed, linens changed for you daily, and $2.1 million in the bank.)

* Buy "interview clothes" with your parents credit card. Display clothes, return clothes, spend cash.

* Convince parents to go on vacation. Sublet house to a family of Scandinavian tourists.

* Convince parents to go on vacation. Run prostitution ring out of the house. Slide across floor in your socks and white underpants while wearing Ray-Bans. Do not join Church of Scientology and potential earnings can be great.

* Write ridiculous manifesto on the virtues of being a social piranha. (This does not actually elicit money, but does give your parents something to tell the rest of the family.)

About the Authors.

Early on in his youth Anthony E. Marsh concluded that, much like the notion of an eternal afterlife, the concept of a weekly paycheck is nothing more than a fraudulent bourgeois fantasy. To date, he has written three screenplays, five magazine articles, twelve greeting cards, and a novel which his mother has praised as, "Vulgarly, savagely, bitterly funny... A subversively witty performance!" Anthony feels confident that sponging is his true calling and is committed to spreading the gospel—he even has plans for a theme park. He was born in Hollywood where he was immediately dropped on his head by an aging doctor with a thing for Thorazine. He still lives a short car ride from his parents.

Jay Blumenfield has been sued by Bozo the Clown, was thrown in the Broward County jail for singing covers of 2 Live Crew songs, and, as mentioned earlier, has never felt the need to help his co-authors proof-read this book. As lead guitarist for the alternative slam-glam-thank-you-ma'am pop band, Too Much Joy, he has released three albums on Warner Bros. Records and has supposedly appeared on such programs as the McLaughlin Report, CBS' The Midnight Hour, CNN, NPR, and MTV News, though nobody we know can remember seeing him. Jay says he's bi-coastal, but his friends think it's just a phase.

As a child, Robert Moritz's ATM and Dishwasher allowed him to star in a commercial for the cult soft-porn film, Chatterbox. Among his other notable accomplishments he has delivered a pizza to Warren Beatty, performed on national television with his speed-ukulele band, Uke Til U Puke, and been paid an inordinate sum of money by GQ magazine to let women smell him. For three consecutive years, he "borrowed" office supplies from Seventeen magazine before moving on to sample lunch bags at The Jane Pratt Show and Tell magazine, where 43 different versions of this book were conveniently photocopied. He lives in New York City.

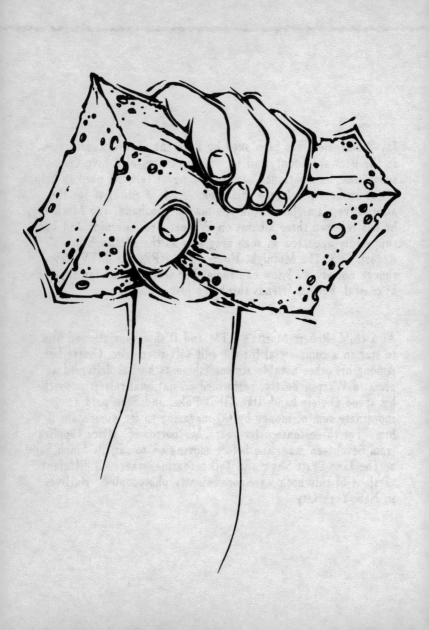